COVER

THE "GREEN VIOLINIST" IS
ONE OF CHAGALL'S PAINTED
MEMORIES OF HIS UNCLE, WHO
FIDDLED, AND OF HIS BIRTHPLACE
IN VITEBSK, RUSSIA.

OIL, 1918
SOLOMON R. GUGGENHEIM MUSEUM, N.Y.

THE FIDDLER, THE VIOLIN, THE
VIOLET CLOTHES, AND THE SOARING
DANCER CREATE A SENSE OF MUSIC THROUGH THE
ARTIST'S USE OF COLOR. THE GREEN FACE AND HAND MAKE
THE OLD TUNE SEEM NEW AS A FRESH GREEN SPRING.
WHILE THE DARK VIOLET COLORS MAY REFLECT THE
SADNESS OF THE
LONG, HARD, RUSSIAN
WINTER, WE ARE
WARMED BY
THE GLOW
FROM THE
ORANGE
VIOLIN.

Permission A D A G P, 1969,
by French Reproduction Rights Inc.

WORLD RIGHTS RESERVED BY ERNEST RABOFF AND GEMINI-SMITH, INC. FIRST PRINTING 1968

ISBN Trade: 0-385-04917-X
Library: 0-385-05125-5

LIBRARY OF CONGRESS CATALOG CARD NO. 68-26549

PRINTED IN JAPAN BY TOPPAN

VASE OF LILIES   MAXWELL GALLERIES, SAN FRANCISCO

DEDICATED TO CATHERINE, STEPHEN, DAVID, CHRISTOPHER, DOROTHY AND ROBERT WILLOUGHBY

MARC CHAGALL

By Ernest Raboff

ART
FOR
CHILDREN

A GEMINI-SMITH BOOK

EDITED BY BRADLEY SMITH

PUBLISHED BY
DOUBLEDAY & CO., INC.

GARDEN CITY, NEW YORK
1968

MARC CHAGALL WAS BORN ON JULY 7, 1887.

HIS BIRTHPLACE WAS A SMALL RUSSIAN VILLAGE CALLED VITEBSK.

ZAHAR CHAGALL, HIS FATHER, WORKED IN A HERRING PACKING HOUSE. HIS SON REMEMBERS HIM AS A TALL, QUIET AND SHY MAN WHO WAS ALWAYS WORKING.

FEIGA-ITA, HIS MOTHER, HAD EIGHT OTHER CHILDREN BESIDES HER OLDEST SON, MARC. SHE HAD A SMALL SHOP IN HER HOME WHERE SHE SOLD HERRING, FLOUR, SUGAR, AND SPICES TO ADD TO THE FAMILY INCOME.

CHAGALL MOVED TO FRANCE IN 1923. FROM 1941 UNTIL 1948, HE LIVED IN THE UNITED STATES. THEN HE RETURNED TO FRANCE, BUT IT WAS THE MEMORIES OF RUSSIA THAT HE PAINTED AND FOR WHICH HE IS MOST FAMOUS.

MARC CHAGALL SAID: "TO KEEP THE EARTH ON ONE'S ROOTS AND FIND ANOTHER EARTH...THAT IS A REAL MIRACLE."

ON **PAINTING** AS A MEANS OF SELF-EXPRESSION: "IT WAS MORE NECESSARY FOR ME THAN FOOD. IT SEEMED TO ME LIKE A WINDOW THROUGH WHICH I COULD HAVE TAKEN FLIGHT TOWARD ANOTHER WORLD."

"AS I GROW OLDER I SEE MORE CLEARLY AND DISTINCTLY WHAT IS **RIGHT** AND **WRONG** IN OUR WAY OF LIFE AND HOW RIDICULOUS IS EVERYTHING NOT ACHIEVED WITH ONE'S OWN BLOOD AND ONE'S OWN SOUL, EVERYTHING NOT INFUSED WITH LOVE."

"EVERYTHING CAN AND WILL BE TRANSFORMED IN LIFE AND IN ART, IF WE SPEAK THE WORD **LOVE** WITHOUT SHAME... IN IT LIES TRUE **ART**..."

PORTRAIT OF THE ARTIST BY RABOFF

"MIDSUMMER NIGHT'S DREAM" IS A PLAY BY WILLIAM SHAKESPEARE IN WHICH A MAN IN LOVE IS TURNED INTO A DONKEY. CHAGALL HAS PAINTED THIS IDEA SHOWING, IN HIS OWN WAY, HOW THE MAN IS CHANGED. EACH OF US CAN ENJOY FINDING THE MEANING FOR OURSELVES IN THIS PAINTING.

ONE FIRST NOTICES THE ANIMAL HEAD ON THE MAN'S BODY, THEN THE DREAM-LIKE FACE OF THE BRIDE. THE RED ANGEL SEEMS TO BE FLYING TOWARD THE HORNS OF THE ANIMAL HEAD. NOTICE HOW THE GLOWING LIGHT OF THE ANGEL BRIGHTLY SHOWS ON THE FLOWERING TREE AND ON THE GREEN FIDDLING CLOWN.

Marc Chagall

CHAGALL MAY BE SAYING THAT MAN, EVEN THOUGH AN ANIMAL, HAS THE ABILITY WITHIN HIM TO BE A CLOWN, A LOVER AND A MUSICIAN.

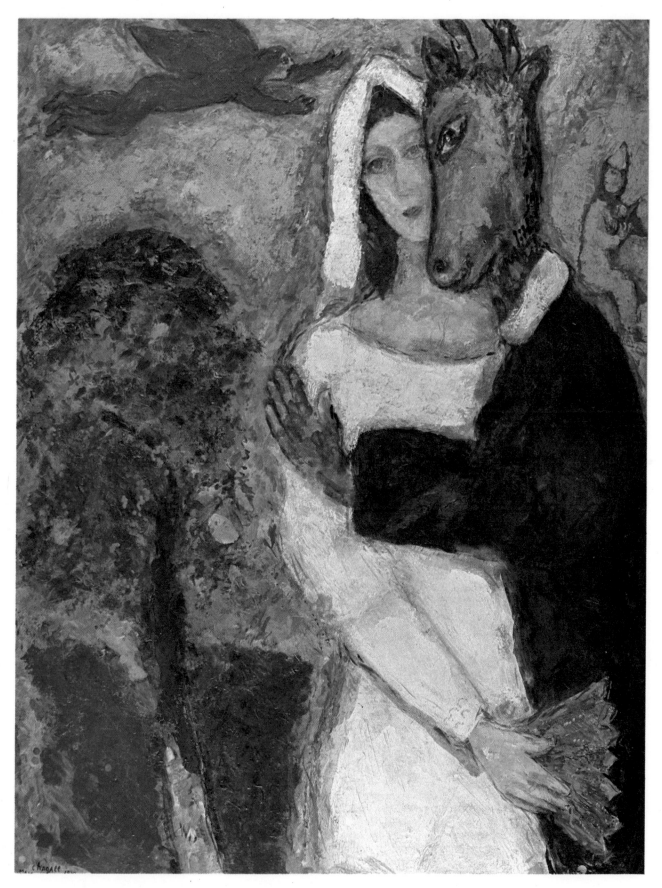

MIDSUMMER NIGHT'S DREAM   1939   MUSEUM OF PAINTING AND SCULPTURE , GRENOBLE , FRANCE

"THE THREE CANDLES" IS A DRAMATIC AND
POWERFUL COMPOSITION. THE CANDLES, THE BRIDE
AND GROOM, THE WOMEN WITH RAISED ARMS BEHIND A
POINTED PICKET FENCE, THE HARLEQUIN STANDING ON A
STOOL—ALL POINT UPWARDS LIKE ROCKETS TOWARDS
THE SKY. AS THOUGH EXPLODING, THEY SHOWER THE
EARTH WITH FLOWERS AND GREEN LEAVES, TUMBLING ANGELS,
AND WITH THE HAPPY VIOLINIST CHAGALL OFTEN PAINTED.

THE BRIDEGROOM, HOLDING HIS WIFE IN HIS ARMS,
LOOKS STARTLED AND AMAZED. THE HOUSES ARE
VERY STILL, AND EVEN THE ANIMAL RESTS
CONTENTEDLY UNDER THE CANDLES.

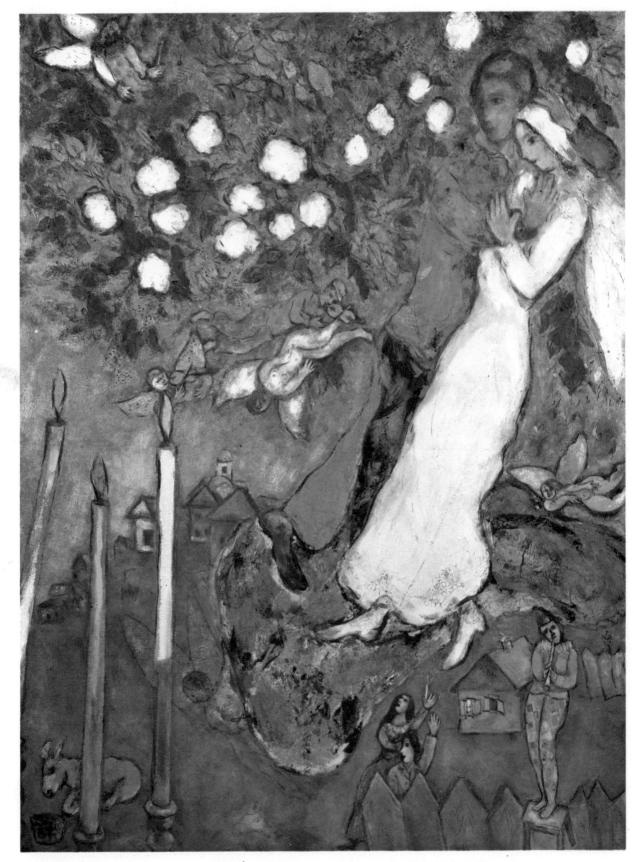

THREE CANDLES   READER'S DIGEST COLLECTION, PLEASANTVILLE, NEW YORK

"I AND THE VILLAGE" IS AS MUCH FUN AS IT IS BEAUTIFUL.

THE EYE OF THE COW, CENTERED IN THE PICTURE, SEES MANY THINGS. WITHIN ITS HEAD IS THE VISION OF ITSELF WITH THE MILKMAID. OUTSIDE ITSELF IT IS AWARE OF A PERSON FACING IT, PERHAPS THE ARTIST.

IN THE LOWER LEFT CORNER THE SUN AND MOON ARE COMBINED AND REPEAT A PATTERN THAT MAKES A DIAGONAL PATH ACROSS THE PICTURE.

IN THE UPPER RIGHT SIDE A PRIEST STANDS IN THE DOORWAY OF HIS CHURCH.

CHAGALL SHOWS US THE VILLAGE FROM MANY POINTS OF VIEW, RIGHT SIDE UP AND UPSIDE DOWN. THE HAPPINESS OF THE ARTIST AND OF THE LIFE OF THE VILLAGE IS SHOWN BY THE COLORFUL BEADS WORN BY THE COW AND THE SMILE ON THE LIPS OF THE PERSON ON THE RIGHT.

I AND THE VILLAGE   1911   THE MUSEUM OF MODERN ART, NEW YORK

CHAGALL'S PAINTING OF "THE POET" IS LIKE A POEM
WRITTEN WITH PICTURES INSTEAD OF WORDS.

THE POSITION OF THE POET'S HEAD IMMEDIATELY ATTRACTS
OUR ATTENTION. LIKE POETS AND PAINTERS, EVERYONE
DAYDREAMS AT TIMES. DO YOU EVER FEEL AS IF
YOUR HEAD AND MIND COULD FLOAT, TWIST, AND TURN
BACKWARDS, SIDEWAYS, OR UPSIDE DOWN? OUR
IMAGINATIONS CAN ALMOST CARRY US AWAY FROM OUR BODIES.

ARTISTS OFTEN TRAIN THEIR MINDS SO THAT THEY
CAN LOSE THEMSELVES IN
THOUGHT WHEREVER THEY
ARE WORKING. IT IS PART OF
THEIR PROFESSION TO SHARE
WITH US THE RESULTS OF
THESE IMAGININGS.

THIS POET SEEMS LOST IN
THOUGHT AS HE SITS WITH
HIS PEN, A CIGARETTE, AND
HIS AFFECTIONATE CAT. THE
FLOWERS OF HIS THINKING
FLOAT NEARBY. THE BLUE SKY
IS REPEATED IN THE BOTTLE
AND HIS CLOTHES. LIKE THE FACETS
OF A DIAMOND, EACH ANGLE
HAS A BEAUTY OF ITS OWN.

THE POET   1911   THE PHILADELPHIA MUSEUM OF ART

IN "THREE ACROBATS" CHAGALL USES FORM WITH COLOR, AND VERY LITTLE LINE TO TELL THE STORY. THE PERFORMING WOMAN IS THE STAR OF THE ACT.

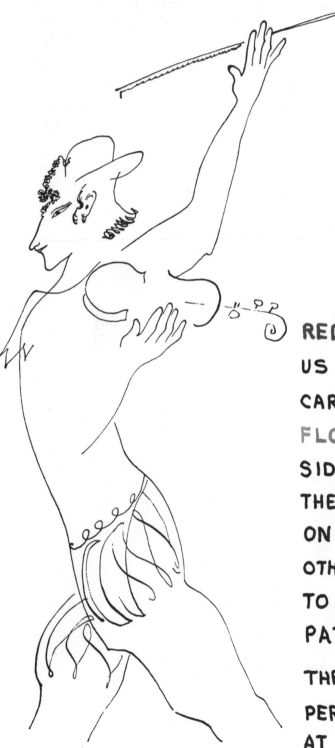

HER HEAD, FRAMED BY HER ARM AND RAISED LEG, ATTRACTS US FIRST. THEN OUR EYES MOVE TO THE OUTSTRETCHED ARM, DOWN THE BLUE CURTAIN, AND TO THE WAITING ACROBAT IN THE RED SHIRT. HIS FEET POINT US ACROSS THE BRIGHT CARPET TO THE BOUQUET OF FLOWERS, THEN UP THE RIGHT SIDE OF THE PICTURE. HERE, THE THIRD ACROBAT, WITH ARM ON HEAD, GUIDES US UP THE OTHER BLUE DECORATED CURTAIN TO COMPLETE THE TRIANGULAR PATTERN.

THE WOMAN'S TWO ASSISTANTS, PERHAPS LIKE US, GAZE IN WONDER AT HER FINE PERFORMANCE.

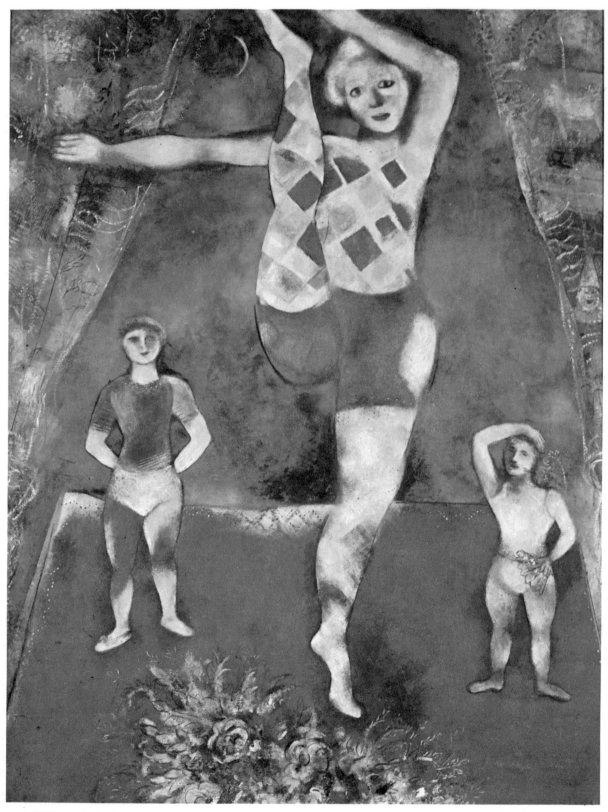

THREE ACROBATS   OIL   S.F. BRODY COLLECTION, LOS ANGELES

"VASE OF FLOWERS" GLOWS LIKE AN OUTDOOR FIRE IN THE BLUE OF THE NIGHT SKY. THE BOUQUET FILLS THE NIGHT WITH COLOR AND FRAGRANCE.

THE SOUNDS OF THE EVENING ARE REPRESENTED BY THE VIOLINIST IN THE UPPER LEFT CORNER.

THE ANIMAL ON THE ROOF SEEMS TO BE A SYMBOL OF SECURITY AND PEACE.

THE MOON IS REFLECTED IN A HALO OF LIGHT AROUND THE RESTING ANIMAL'S HEAD.

VASE OF FLOWERS, BY MOONLIGHT 1943   MRS. BEATRICE GLASS, NEW YORK

"PARIS THROUGH A WINDOW" IS A COLORFUL AND EXCITING PAINTING. CHAGALL ENJOYED DRAWING SCENES OF PARIS AND ITS LANDMARKS SUCH AS THE EIFFEL TOWER. HE NEVER TIRED OF LOOKING AT AND PAINTING THIS QUEEN OF CITIES.

THE TWO LOVERS WALK CLOSE TOGETHER AND THE ARTIST HAS PAINTED THEM HEAD TO HEAD. THE UPSIDE DOWN TRAIN IS PART OF CHAGALL'S PARIS SCENE. IT PUFFS A COLUMN OF SMOKE LIKE A SIGNATURE ACROSS THE STREETS.

ABOVE , A MAN WAVES A FLAG. THE BUILDINGS REFLECT THE LIGHTS OF THE SKY, WHILE THE SKY CATCHES THE GLOW OF THE FRENCH CITY.

THE WINDOW FRAME MIRRORS THE MANY COLORS SEEN OUTSIDE.

THE CAT, PAINTED WITH HUMAN FEATURES, IS A GOOD FRIEND AND COMPANION.

PARIS THROUGH A WINDOW   SOLOMON R. GUGGENHEIM MUSEUM, NEW YORK

CHAGALL SHOWS US IN "THE ACROBAT" HOW UNUSUALLY LONG THE ARMS, BODIES, AND LEGS OF THESE ENTERTAINERS APPEAR TO BE AS THEY PERFORM THEIR AMAZING FEATS.

IN THE FRENCH CIRCUSES, THE ACROBATS DRESS IN COSTUMES OF CLOWNS OR HARLEQUINS. THEY RESEMBLE PINWHEELS OF FLASHING COLORS AS THEY DIVE THROUGH HOOPS, DO BACKFLIPS, AND A SERIES OF SOMERSAULTS.

THE ARTIST MAKES ACROBATS OF OUR EYES ALSO. OUR ATTENTION MOVES IN CIRCLES AS WE LOOK FROM THE HEAD TO THE RUFFLED COLLAR, THE ARMS, THE HOOP, COSTUME, AND FINALLY TO THE RUNNING LEGS.

EVEN THE DESIGNS AND PATTERNS OF THE COSTUME EXPRESS A FEELING OF ACTION AND MOVEMENT.

THE ACROBAT   1914   ALBRIGHT-KNOX ART GALLERY , BUFFALO

"PEASANT LIFE" IS THE STORY OF A SMALL VILLAGE TOLD FOR US IN PAINT BY A GREAT STORYTELLER. CHAGALL SHOWS THE PLEASANT EVERYDAY LIFE OF THE VILLAGE'S RURAL PEOPLE.

NOTICE THE FARMER'S WELL-FED HORSE. THIS IS THE PEASANT'S MOST IMPORTANT FELLOW WORKER AS WELL AS HIS LOVED COMPANION.

THE COTTAGE, WITH ITS WINDOWS AND SHUTTERS, THE GAS LANTERN, AND THE TREE FORM THE SETTING FOR THIS PICTURE-STORY. THE HORSE AND CART ARE READY TO TAKE THE VILLAGE FAMILY WITH THEIR MANY FARM PRODUCTS TO MARKET.

THE DANCING COUPLE COMPLETES CHAGALL'S COLORFUL PICTURE OF PEASANT LIFE.

PEASANT LIFE   ALBRIGHT - KNOX ART GALLERY , BUFFALO

IN "THE BIRTHDAY" CHAGALL SHOWS US HOW HE FELT ON ONE OF HIS BIRTHDAYS. IN THE PICTURE, AS IN HIS MEMORY, HE FLOATS INTO THE HOME OF BELLA, HIS FUTURE BRIDE. SHE GREETS HIM WITH A BOUQUET OF FLOWERS AND A KISS.

HER DRESS AND ONE FOOT ARE CAUGHT UP IN THE BREEZE OF THE ARTIST'S MOTION.

HER PURSE LIES ON THE TABLE IN FRONT OF THE CAKE SHE HAS BAKED. BESIDE IT IS A GLASS FOR WINE AND A PIECE OF WATERMELON.

THE BRIGHT RED OF THE FLOOR, THE TABLE, AND THE BEDSPREAD ADDS A WARM GLOW TO THE ROOM.

THROUGH THE WINDOW WE CAN SEE THE QUIET STREET, THE NEIGHBOR'S PICKET FENCE AND THE STARS IN THE EVENING SKY.

CHAGALL HAS PAINTED HIS JOYOUS BIRTHDAY MEMORY FOR EVERYONE TO SHARE.

THE BIRTHDAY , 1915   THE MUSEUM OF MODERN ART , NEW YORK

ONE SHOULD STUDY "TIME IS A RIVER WITHOUT BANKS"
TO EXPLORE THE FULL MEANING OF THE TITLE.

THE CURIOUS FLYING
FISH PLAYING THE
VIOLIN REFLECTS THE
COLOR AND FLAMES OF
THE SUN ON ITS WINGS
AND MOUTH.

ON ONE BANK OF THE
RIVER A YOUNG COUPLE
IS UNAWARE OF GRANDFATHER TIME TICKING AWAY
THE HOURS. THEY HEAR ONLY THE MUSIC.

ON THE OTHER SIDE, CURVING AROUND THE HORIZON
ARE THE HOUSES OF THE CITY. THEY STAND SILENTLY,
HOLDING THE HISTORY OF TIME AND THE RIVER
IN THEIR WORN BRICKS AND STONE WALLS.

THE BLUE OF THE
DAY AND THE DARKER
BLUE OF NIGHT
FILL THE CANVAS
WITH COLOR.

A LONE FISHERMAN
PADDLES HIS WAY
INTO THE FUTURE.

TIME IS A RIVER WITHOUT BANKS   THE MUSEUM OF MODERN ART, NEW YORK

"THE FIDDLER" WHO PLAYS HIS VIOLIN IN MANY OF CHAGALL'S PAINTINGS WAS IN REALITY A FAVORITE UNCLE. THE ARTIST KNEW OF THE FAMOUS RUSSIAN STORY BY SHOLEM ALEICHEM ABOUT A FIDDLER WHO PLAYED FROM THE ROOF TOPS. IN THIS PICTURE, CHAGALL PLACED HIS FIDDLER WITH ONE FOOT ON THE ROOF. WHEN THE FIDDLER PLAYED IT WAS AS THOUGH HE WERE DANCING ABOVE THE ROOFS AND AS IF HIS MUSIC TOOK HIM UP AMONG THE ANGELS, CLOSE TO HEAVEN.

TO SHOW THAT HE ENJOYED HIS MUSICAL UNCLE WHILE HE WAS SMALL, WHEN HE WAS GROWING UP, AND WHEN HE

WAS A YOUNG MAN, CHAGALL PAINTED HIMSELF WITH THREE HEADS IN THE LOWER LEFT SIDE OF THE PICTURE.

THE HOUSES ARE ALL LIGHTED EITHER FROM WITHIN OR FROM WITHOUT AS THOUGH THE PEOPLE MIGHT BE LISTENING TO THE MUSIC IN THE NIGHT.

IN THE LOWER RIGHT CORNER SOME OF THE BIRDS ALSO LISTEN WHILE OTHERS SEEM TO BE SINGING WITH THE FIDDLER.

VIOLINIST   OIL, 1912-13   STEDELIJK MUSEUM, AMSTERDAM